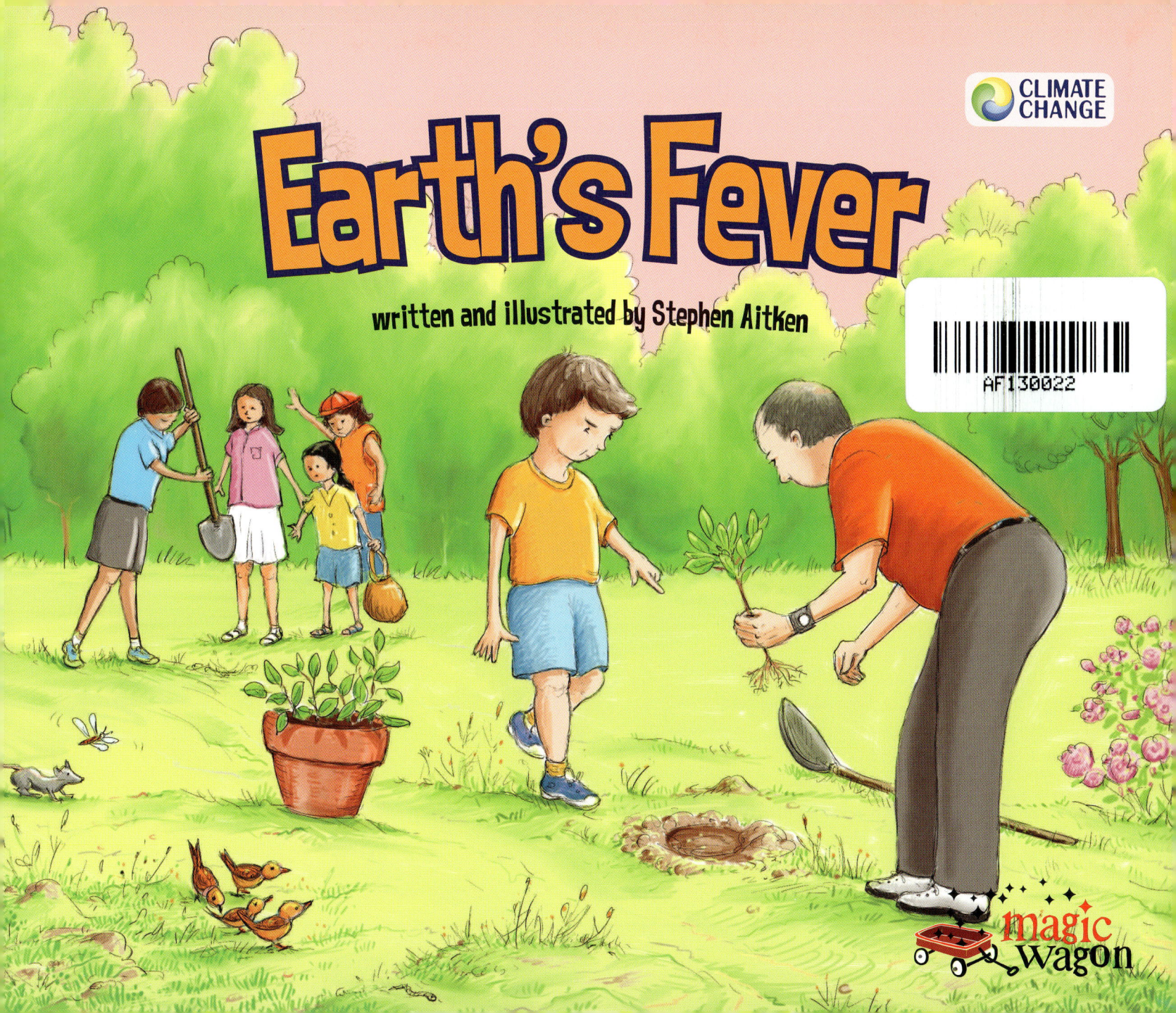

visit us at www.abdopublishing.com

Published by Magic Wagon, a division of the ABDO Group, 8000 West 78th Street, Edina, Minnesota 55439. Copyright © 2012 by Abdo Consulting Group, Inc. International copyrights reserved in all countries. All rights reserved. No part of this book may be reproduced in any form without written permission from the publisher.

Looking Glass Library™ is a trademark and logo of Magic Wagon.

Printed in the United States of America, North Mankato, Minnesota.
052011
092011
This book contains at least 10% recycled materials.

Written and Illustrated by Stephen Aitken
Edited by Stephanie Hedlund and Rochelle Baltzer
Cover and interior layout and design by Abbey Fitzgerald

Library of Congress Cataloging-in-Publication Data

Aitken, Stephen, 1953-
  Earth's fever / written and illustrated by Stephen Aitken.
    p. cm. -- (Climate change)
  Includes index.
  ISBN 978-1-61641-670-6
  1. Greenhouse effect, Atmospheric--Juvenile literature. 2. Carbon dioxide--Juvenile literature. 3. Global warming--Juvenile literature. I. Title.
  QC912.3. A38 2012
  363.738'74--dc22
                                         2011001872

Contents

Earth Has a Fever... 4
Who Turned On the Greenhouse Gas?................... 9
Climate Change and People 14
How to Cure Earth's Fever................................ 20
Did You Know?... 28
Dr. Know Recycles!.. 29
What Can You Do?.. 30
Glossary 31
Web Sites... 31
Index.. 32

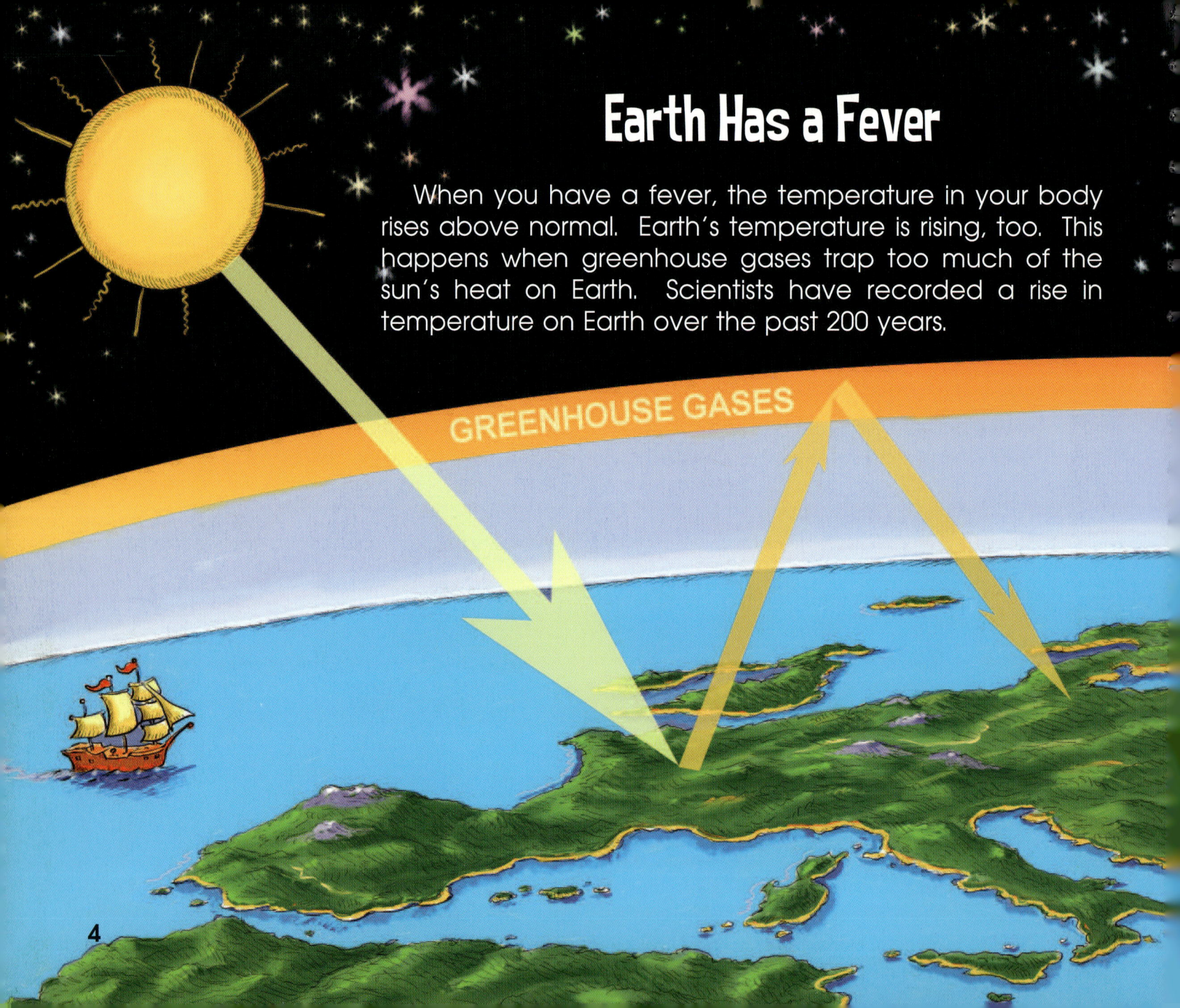

Earth Has a Fever

When you have a fever, the temperature in your body rises above normal. Earth's temperature is rising, too. This happens when greenhouse gases trap too much of the sun's heat on Earth. Scientists have recorded a rise in temperature on Earth over the past 200 years.

GREENHOUSE GASES

HOT FACT: Greenhouse gases trap the sun's heat in Earth's atmosphere. This is called the greenhouse effect. With more carbon dioxide (CO_2) in the air, it is harder for heat to escape. The trapped heat is giving Earth a fever!

HOT FACT: In the last 60 years, Earth's average temperature has risen almost one and a half degrees!

HOT FACT: Half the electricity used in the United States comes from power plants that burn coal. More CO_2 is produced per person in the United States than in almost any other country in the world.

Who Turned On the Greenhouse Gas?

Power plants that burn coal produce a lot of carbon. Cars and trucks that run on oil and gas cause greenhouse gas levels to rise even further.

Cutting down forests produces carbon, too. People cut forests for lumber and burn them to clear land for farms and houses. Close to half of Earth's natural forests have been lost. Fewer forests means more CO_2 remains in the air.

COOL IDEA: China is planting the world's largest human-made forest. It will have more than 50 billion trees when it is completed.

Methane is another important greenhouse gas. Livestock, such as cattle, pigs, and sheep, produce high levels of methane. This adds to the greenhouse gas layer in the atmosphere as well.

Climate Change and People

Rising temperatures are creating changes in global climate patterns. Some places are becoming colder while others are getting warmer. That's why global warming is not the correct name for Earth's fever. Extreme weather events, like hurricanes, tornadoes, floods, and droughts are getting stronger and happening more often. This is climate change.

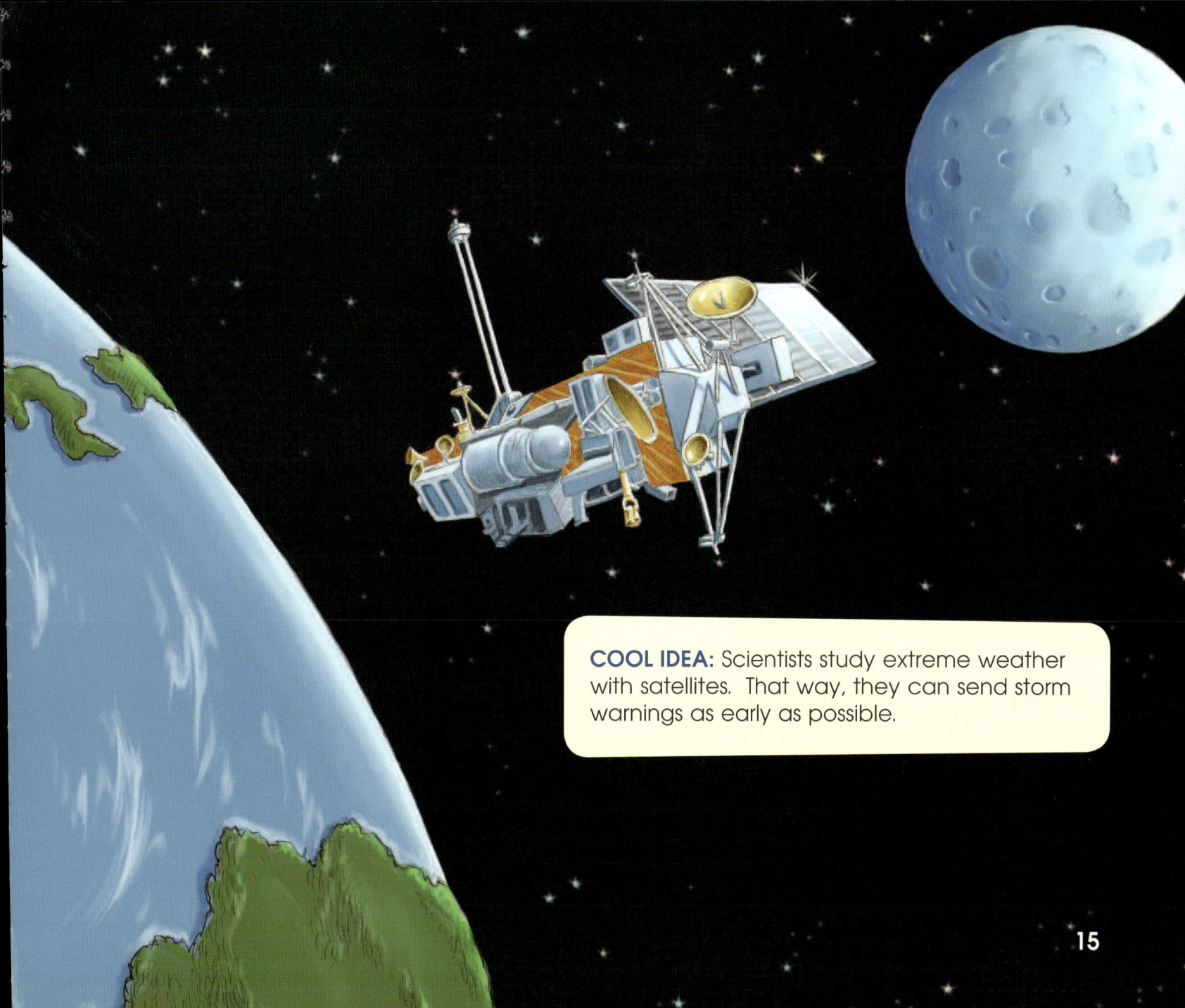

COOL IDEA: Scientists study extreme weather with satellites. That way, they can send storm warnings as early as possible.

Almost 7 billion people live on Earth. Scientists expect that there will be up to 10 billion by the year 2050. More people will produce more carbon and use more fossil fuels. At the same time, flooding and rising sea levels are reducing the amount of land that people can live on.

Mountain glaciers provide water for many rivers. As temperatures keep rising, glaciers are becoming smaller. Many rivers now have more water in the spring and less in the summer when it is needed for crops.

HOT FACT: By 2050, several billion people could face a water and food shortage.

How to Cure Earth's Fever

The only real cure for Earth's fever is to lower the amount of carbon in the atmosphere. Renewable energy sources must replace the burning of fossil fuels. Types of energy that do not give off carbon include solar, wind, geothermal, wave, and tidal power. These will help create a new energy balance on Earth.

COOL IDEA: The use of wind power is increasing rapidly all over the world. Many wind turbines grouped together make a wind farm.

Trees take CO_2 from the air and give off oxygen. Planting trees can help lower CO_2 in the atmosphere and affect the climate. Some communities get together to plant trees. Are there places to plant trees in your neighborhood? What about your own backyard?

To help reduce carbon, people can buy cars that produce fewer greenhouse gases. There are now hybrid cars that use both gas and battery power. Electric cars don't use any fossil fuels.

You can help save the world by keeping your carbon footprint small. Shut off lights when you leave a room. And, turn down the heat in the winter and air conditioning in the summer.

COOL IDEA: You can calculate your carbon footprint to see how much CO_2 you produce each day with a Climate Change Calculator online. By reducing CO_2, we can keep the planet healthy for everyone.

Did You Know?

People breathe out two pounds (1 kg) of CO_2 every day.

Temperatures are expected to rise even more this century if we don't change how we live. Scientist expect average temperatures to become anywhere from three degrees Fahrenheit (1.7°C) to seven degrees Fahrenheit (3.9°C) warmer than they are now.

About 20% of the electricity produced in the United States is from nuclear power plants. The safe storage of nuclear waste and the danger of leakage at the plants is a problem.

Animal manure (poop!) can be burned in special power plants to produce energy.

Because of climate change, the glaciers in Glacier National Park in Montana could be gone in 30 years!

Dr. Know Recycles!

The fewer things we put in the garbage, the smaller the landfill will be. Recycling uses less energy and produces fewer greenhouse gases. Is there a recycling program at your school? Do you recycle at home?

A recycle bin may have separate places for aluminum cans, paper, and glass. Follow the rules written on the recycle container your community provides. Recyclable items are taken to a materials recovery facility, or an MRF (pronounced 'murf'). There, they are sorted and then tied together in big bundles. The bundles are sold to manufacturers who use them to make new products.

What you need:

- A pen
- Paper

What to do:
For each item on the list below, write down three ways you can reuse it.

- Cardboard box
- Carpet ends
- Empty paint can
- Glass jar
- Mop handle
- Newspapers
- Plastic bag
- Twist ties

What Can You Do?

The change in Earth's temperature is almost totally due to human activities. Burning oil and gas for cars, trucks, and buses releases gases that trap heat on Earth. The power used to create electricity and other forms of energy adds to the problem. Here are a few things you can do to help keep the temperature from rising more!

Make your neighborhood beautiful and reduce climate change by planting trees and other plants.

Learn! Read more books about climate change. Then tell people about what you learned.

Recycle as much as you can to help reduce the amount of garbage in landfills.

Talk to your teacher and classmates about how your class can reduce its carbon footprint. Can you start a recycling program at school? Could you start a clean-up night? Get the whole class involved in saving the planet!

Glossary

atmosphere - the layer of gas surrounding Earth.

carbon dioxide (CO_2) - a heavy, colorless gas that is formed when fuel containing the element carbon is burned.

carbon footprint - the amount of carbon produced by someone's activities.

climate - the weather and temperatures that are normal in a certain place.

fossil fuels - oil, gas, and coal found deep in the ground. Fossil fuels are burned by people for the energy they release.

geothermal - of or related to using heat found deep in the ground.

glacier - a large body of ice moving slowly down or across land.

greenhouse gas - a gas, such as carbon dioxide, that traps heat in Earth's atmosphere.

methane - a colorless, odorless, flammable gas used as a fuel. It forms when organic matter breaks down.

renewable energy - energy that can be replaced naturally. Renewable energy resources include wind energy and solar energy.

Web Sites

To learn more about climate change, visit ABDO Group online at **www.abdopublishing.com**. Web sites about climate change are featured on our Book Links page. These links are routinely monitored and updated to provide the most current information available.

Index

A

animals 5, 13

B

Bangladesh 17

C

carbon 6, 9, 10, 16, 20, 24
carbon dioxide 5, 6, 8, 10, 22, 27
carbon footprint 26, 27
China 11

E

electric cars 24

F

forests 10, 11, 13, 23
fossil fuels 8, 9, 16, 20

G

glaciers 18
greenhouse gas 4, 5, 6, 9, 13, 24

H

hybrid cars 24

O

oxygen 6, 22

P

people 16, 17, 19

plants 5, 11, 18, 22
power plants 8, 9

R

renewable energy 20, 21

S

scientists 4, 15, 16
spring 18
summer 18, 26

T

temperatures 4, 7, 14, 18

W

weather 14, 15